Ocean Animals

# Sea Turtles

by Christina Leaf

BELLWETHER MEDIA
MINNEAPOLIS, MN

**Blastoff! Beginners** are developed by literacy experts and educators to meet the needs of early readers. These engaging informational texts support young children as they begin reading about their world. Through simple language and high frequency words paired with crisp, colorful photos, Blastoff! Beginners launch young readers into the universe of independent reading.

Blastoff! Universe ★

Reading Level

Grade K

Grades 1-3

Grade 4

BLASTOFF! DISCOVERY

## Sight Words in This Book 🔍

| a | help | on | they |
|------|------|-------|------|
| are | is | the | to |
| big | it | them | who |
| for | look | then | |
| from | many | there | |
| have | of | these | |

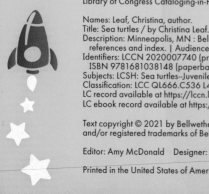

This edition first published in 2021 by Bellwether Media, Inc.

No part of this publication may be reproduced in whole or in part without written permission of the publisher. For information regarding permission, write to Bellwether Media, Inc., Attention: Permissions Department, 6012 Blue Circle Drive, Minnetonka, MN 55343.

Library of Congress Cataloging-in-Publication Data

Names: Leaf, Christina, author.
Title: Sea turtles / by Christina Leaf.
Description: Minneapolis, MN : Bellwether Media, Inc., 2021. | Series: Ocean animals | Includes bibliographical references and index. | Audience: Grades PreK-2
Identifiers: LCCN 2020007740 (print) | LCCN 2020007741 (ebook) | ISBN 9781644873274 (library binding) | ISBN 9781681038148 (paperback) | ISBN 9781681037905 (ebook)
Subjects: LCSH: Sea turtles--Juvenile literature.
Classification: LCC QL666.C536 L428 2021 (print) | LCC QL666.C536 (ebook) | DDC 597.92/8--dc23
LC record available at https://lccn.loc.gov/2020007740
LC ebook record available at https://lccn.loc.gov/2020007741

Editor: Amy McDonald   Designer: Andrea Schneider

Printed in the United States of America, North Mankato, MN.

# Table of Contents

# Sea Turtles!

Who is on
the move?
It is a sea turtle!

There are
many kinds
of sea turtles.

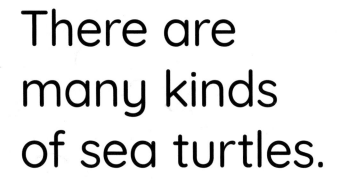

leatherback

green

hawksbill

Sea turtles are
super swimmers.
They travel far!

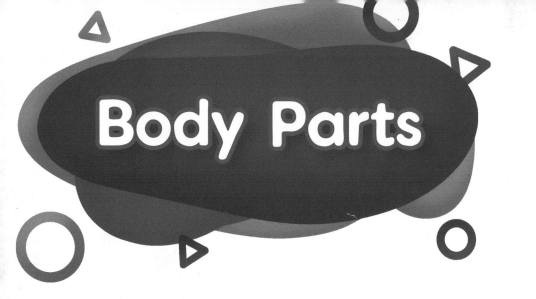

# Body Parts

Sea turtles
have big shells.
Shells keep
them safe.

shell

Sea turtles have **flippers**. These help turtles swim.

flipper

Sea turtles have **beaks**. Beaks help them bite food.

beak

# A Long Trip

Sea turtles swim
far from home.
They look
for food.

Sea turtles **return** home.
Then females lay
eggs on a beach.

eggs

female

Baby turtles **hatch** from eggs. Back to the sea!

hatching

# Sea Turtle Facts

## Sea Turtle Body Parts

shell

flipper

beak

## Sea Turtle Food

jellyfish

seaweed

crabs

22

# Glossary

**beaks**

the mouths of
sea turtles

**flippers**

wide, flat body
parts turtles use
to swim

**hatch**

to break out of
an egg

**return**

to come back
to something

# To Learn More

## ON THE WEB

### FACTSURFER

Factsurfer.com gives you a safe, fun way to find more information.

1. Go to www.factsurfer.com.

2. Enter "sea turtles" into the search box and click 🔍.

3. Select your book cover to see a list of related content.

## Index

The images in this book are reproduced through the courtesy of: Richard Whitcombe, front cover; Rich Carey, pp. 3, 7 (green); Daniel Wilhelm Nilsson, pp. 4-5; Willyam Bradberry, pp. 6-7; catalinaug, p. 6; Nature Photo, p. 7 (hawksbill); Davdeka, pp. 8-9; Kjeld Friss, pp. 10-11; Michael Smith ITWP, pp. 12-13; Durden Images, pp. 14-15 (beak); Chai Seamaker, pp. 14-15; Shane Myers Photography, pp. 16-17, 23 (flippers); Kalaeva, p. 18 (eggs); David Evison, pp. 18-19; Wild Wonders of Europe/ Zankl/ Minden, p. 20; VTinoco, pp. 20-21; Nerthuz, p. 22 (parts); Pawel Kalisinski Pexels, p. 22 (jellyfish); Allexxandar, p. 22 (seaweed); Kondratuk Aleksei, p. 22 (crabs); Durden Images, p. 23 (beaks); Jason Edwards/ National Geographic Images, p. 23 (hatch); fotopanorama360, p. 23 (return).